I0177449

THE
PROPHET'S
REWARD

Harrison House Books by Joseph Z

THE
PROPHET'S REWARD

PARTNERING WITH
THE PROPHETIC FOR
YOUR FAITH, FAVOR,
AND FINANCIAL
MIRACLES

JOSEPH Z

© Copyright 2025– Joseph Z

Printed in the United States of America. All rights reserved. No portion of this book may be reproduced, stored in a retrieval system, or transmitted in any form or by any means—electronic, mechanical, photocopy, recording, scanning, or other—except for brief quotations in critical reviews or articles, without the prior written permission of the publisher. Unless otherwise identified, Scripture quotations are taken from the New King James Version. Copyright © 1982 by Thomas Nelson, Inc. Used by permission. All rights reserved. Scripture quotation marked KJV is from the King James Version. All emphasis within Scripture quotations is the author's own.

Published by Harrison House Publishers
Shippensburg, PA 17257

ISBN 13 TP: 978-1-6675-1195-5
ISBN 13 eBook: 978-1-6675-1196-2

For Worldwide Distribution
1 2 3 4 5 6 7 8 / 29 28 27 26 25

CONTENTS

1

THE PROPHET'S REWARD

He who receives a prophet in the name of a prophet shall receive a prophet's reward....
—Matthew 10:41

The days are approaching when God's people will need a revelation of His supernatural provision, unlike any time in modern history. Woven throughout the biblical narrative are moments in time of great difficulty and significant intervention. God has used prophets to create an avenue of supernatural provision, protection, and guidance, which interrupted dark agendas being marshaled against His people.

EZEKIEL AND THE VALLEY OF DRY BONES

God will speak through His prophets to release His word, for His Voice is a multiplier. Ezekiel 37 speaks of the valley of dry bones. God asked Ezekiel what he saw then commanded him to prophesy to the bones as He commanded.

With each prophetic command, life advanced. Finally, an exceedingly great army stood before the prophet.

A MAN OR WOMAN WITH A REVELATION FROM GOD IS NEVER AT THE MERCY OF A CULTURE GONE MAD!

Prophets in the right place, at the right time, and under the instruction of God will cause life and will stand against darkness, death, and destruction. Power occurs when the Voice of God comes through the office gift to declare a way when everything seems impossible. Prophets walk in revelation.

Aligning with a legitimate prophet causes an increase. For the Voice of God is a multiplier and *calls those things which be not as though they are* (*see* Romans 4:17). Prophets walk in an office that demonstrates this.

THE PROPHET'S REWARD

The "prophet's reward" can be several things. Some commentators suggest it is a teacher giving a lesson or a preacher giving a great sermon. Although the commentators may be partially correct, they are incomplete; because when we look at the context, Matthew 10:41 doesn't only say prophets, it also speaks of a righteous man's reward.

> *He who receives you receives Me, and he who receives Me receives Him who sent Me.* [41] *He who receives a prophet in the name of a prophet shall receive a prophet's reward. And he who receives a righteous man in the name of a righteous man shall receive a righteous man's reward.* [42] *And whoever gives one of these little ones only a cup of cold water in the name of a disciple, assuredly, I say to you, he shall by no means lose his reward.*
>
> —Matthew 10:40-42

REWARDS ASSOCIATED WITH SPECIFIC INDIVIDUALS

There is more than one classification of a reward as it relates to a specific individual. When the text is specific to a particular individual, it points to a reward based on who that individual is and the honor they receive. When it says prophet, it means prophet. When it says righteous man, it means righteous man. When the text says in the name of a disciple, that is what it means.

We will focus on the prophet *in the name of a prophet*. In other words, for the prophet's reward to engage, they must first be honored and received as legitimate prophets.

HONOR ENGAGES
THE PROPHET'S REWARD

It should be said that honor is what engages the prophet's reward. The *level* of honor given to the office will likely be the same *level* of reward that will come through the office in return.

> *And he said to him, "Look now, there is in this city a man of God, and he is an honorable man; all that he says surely comes to pass. So let us go there; perhaps he can show us the way that we should go."* [7] *Then Saul said to his servant, "But look, if we go, what shall we bring the man? For the bread in our vessels is all gone, and there is no present to bring to the man of God. What do we have?"* [8] *And the servant answered Saul again and said, "Look, I have here at hand one-fourth of a shekel of silver. I will give that to the man of God, to tell us our way."* [9] *(Formerly in Israel,*

when a man went to inquire of God, he spoke thus: "Come, let us go to the seer"; for he who is now called a prophet was formerly called a seer.) [10] *Then Saul said to his servant, "Well said; come, let us go." So, they went to the city where the man of God was.*

—1 Samuel 9:6-10

Saul heard of a seer who could tell him what he needed to know about his lost donkeys. The seer prophet that Saul went to find was Samuel. Notice how they brought a gift with them. It was what they had. He wasn't there to buy a prophecy, as that is always wrong, and anyone who teaches that you must give to receive a prophetic word is also wrong. The gift Saul presented to Samuel was out of honor.

SAMUEL'S OBEDIENCE SAVES ISRAEL

Earlier, Samuel's obedience radically saved Israel from a military takeover. Interestingly, only a few chapters before this moment, Samuel is shown giving sacrifices to the Lord as the Philistines prepared to invade the land! A significant but often overlooked point is that God interrupted the Philistine army's progress as it began to move in!

Now when the Philistines heard that the children of Israel had gathered together at Mizpah, the lords of the Philistines went up against Israel. And when the children of Israel heard of it, they were afraid of the Philistines. [8] So the children of Israel said to Samuel, "Do not cease to cry out to the Lord our God for us, that He may save us from the hand of the Philistines." [9] And Samuel took a suckling lamb and offered it as a whole burnt offering to the Lord. Then Samuel cried out to the Lord for Israel, and the Lord answered him. [10] Now as Samuel was offering up the burnt offering, the Philistines drew near to battle against Israel. But the Lord thundered with a loud thunder upon the Philistines that day, and so confused them that they were overcome before Israel.

—1 Samuel 7:7-10

THE LORD THUNDERED ON THE PHILISTINES

This fulfilled a prophecy spoken by Samuel's mother, Hannah, in 1 Samuel 2:10, saying, "The adversaries of the Lord shall be broken in pieces; from heaven He will thunder against them."

Historian Josephus said God responded to the Philistines with lightning, which flashed in their faces, and shook their weapons out of their hands so that they fled disarmed, and with an earthquake that caused gaps in the earth, into which they fell. The Philistines were disturbed, frightened, and thrown into confusion and disorder. Many of them were destroyed by this thundering of God against them.

The Philistines were smitten before Israel, meaning even though the Philistines fled before Israel, it was not Israel who killed them! Before Israel could even come out against them to fight with them, the Philistines were smitten and destroyed, many of them by the thunder and lightning and by the earth opening upon them and devouring them![1]

When God thundered, I can only imagine the enemy's face lit up with lightning flashes, and when God roared at them, it sounded like thunder, much like on Mount Sinai (*see* Exodus 19). Can you imagine it? If there was lightning and the ground was opening to swallow the enemies each time He thundered, I imagine every time He spoke—boulders and rocks must have exploded at His thunderous roar! It must

---

[1] Josephus, *The Antiquities of the Jews*, l. 6. c. 2. sect. 2.

have been terrifying for anyone near this display of God's jealousy over His people!

Again, this is part of the prophet's reward—intense levels of protection.

GOD'S BEST WAS TO RULE THROUGH SAMUEL

God was the overseer of Israel, and working with His prophet Samuel, the foreign enemies didn't stand a chance! As shocking as this might be, God's best and highest desire was to work with the prophet and His nation directly. God didn't want to put a king over the nation. He wanted to be their God and lead the people through His prophet!

Sadly, the nation and its people cried out for a king. Like the other heathen nations, they wanted kingly representation to have a king go to battle on their behalf.

It is amazing and tragic that God offered His best and was their greatest Defender, yet the human heart desires to trust in its mechanisms. Even more astonishing is that God told Samuel to tell the people what it would cost them to have a king rather than to have Him rule with a prophet, and they still chose to follow the path of the heathen nations.

A GLIMPSE OF THE PROPHET'S REWARD

This narrative provides a glimpse of the prophet's reward. God, working through the office of the prophet, caused national protection and provision. The people honored Samuel, and Samuel honored God, resulting in God Himself thundering against the enemy of His people!

What could have been if the people had continued with God ruling the nation, with the prophet and the reward working for them? Unlike anything in Scripture, they would likely have been an unstoppable force of protection and provision. The prophet's reward would have been immense protection and provision over the nation. Receiving Samuel as a prophet whom God ordained would have continued the intense protection by God Himself, just as when He stopped the Philistines by thunder!

After God and the prophet stopped the invasion of Israel, the people requested a king—God gave them what they wanted. This story teaches a powerful lesson: God sometimes answers the requests of His people even if they are not entirely what He wants. What an amazing God we serve!

2

SOWING WITH PROPER MOTIVE INDUCES REWARD

Sowing has to do with the heart, not the amounts given. When it comes to sowing, honor always has to do with motive and what the gift means to the one giving it.

IF IT DOESN'T MEAN MUCH TO THE GIVER, IT MIGHT NOT HAVE MUCH IMPACT WITH GOD.

However, if what you give gets your attention, you are more likely to engage the reward. Why is that? Because what you sow has to do with the heart. If your heart is moved, you will know it! You will also know when you have been truly generous, as you will not forget the offering you gave for some time! It will stick with you in your heart!

RADICAL GIVING

Heather and I have often emptied our entire bank accounts to give to a man or woman of God in this manner, specifically into the office of the prophet, which has induced tremendous results over the years. We had sown when there was zero backup and no promise of anything coming in after we gave it all away.

SOWING ACTIVATES GOD'S ECONOMY

Once, during a meeting, when we received a prophetic impartation, we gave the last of what we had and even added to it when more finances came our way following the meeting. At the same time, we gave our car away! We gave so much during those days that we faced ridicule for our actions. We experienced an awakening to the importance of giving and needed to act on it. God's economy is activated by sowing.

YOU CANNOT OUTGIVE GOD

We were broke during those days but had a revelation of honor through giving and would always hear, "You can't outgive God!" I said, "True, but most people never try." We weren't being impulsive or reckless; we had legitimately meditated on giving with honor so much that it changed our lives!

On one occasion, we had one hundred dollars to our name. We agreed that we wouldn't even check with the other if we decided to give. In this meeting, with hundreds of people in attendance, I was overcome with the desire to sow everything we had. I looked to my right to see if Heather agreed, and when I did, she wasn't there! She was already walking forward with a check!

This was one of those churches with security that resembled the Secret Service, which I appreciate because they keep us safe at times today!

HEATHER'S RISKY OFFERING

As Heather walked up the middle aisle with the check in her hand, I remember thinking, *You're too far, too close to the front!* As I looked down from the balcony where I was seated, I thought, *They're going to take you down to the floor!* I watched as my petite, fiery wife boldly walked to the front in this huge meeting venue filled with people, ascended the platform stairs, and slapped our check on the podium!

No one took her down! She sowed our last hundred dollars. Following that meeting, a person approached us and gave us a few hundred dollars.

SOWING AND REWARD

Not long after that season, we began to have resources and cars. We graduated from giving one hundred dollars—a lot of money—to regularly giving one thousand dollars, which was an unbelievable stretch of faith in those days. We would do anything the Lord prompted us to do.

We came to the point where we sowed far more than we could have ever imagined, and we have done it repeatedly and with honor. We know it has been through radical giving that meant something to us, each time, to such a level that we would sweat from concern and yet rejoice simultaneously!

GOD, YOU HAVE A PROBLEM!

If the Lord tells us to give, we don't flinch. When we have issues, we give or tithe according to the value of the issue and say, "Wow, it looks like You have a problem, God!" We mean it when we say that. When we sow in the middle of difficulty, we intentionally make God responsible for our problem.

PROPHETS CARRY INCREASE

We learned that specific ministries have much more increase on them than others, especially the office of the prophet. It might shock you that prophetic ministry isn't just those who stand up and predict what is to come. It isn't always about those who can prophesy to people on an individual level.

Sometimes the office of the prophet is a ministry that broadcasts or has a voice and a special message for this season. Prophets may be pastors, but they typically do the impossible after intense seasons of persecution. Prophets mobilize the troops and give marching orders. They deliver notably powerful teaching as well as revelatory insights.

Sowing into a fully operational prophetic office with honor and joy will engage the prophet's reward. We learned this, and it has been life-changing.

3

ALL SOIL IS NOT THE SAME

All the giving is from a heart of honor and a desire to sow into God's economy. The most potent seed we have ever sown was into the legitimate office of the prophet, working in faith and flowing in the legitimate power of God, giving to prophets who have a revelation about increase and are massive givers themselves.

All soil is not the same. When we have given under the leading of the Spirit into the right kind of soil, with our hearts in the right place, there have been explosive results in our lives and ministry!

Supernatural resources have repeatedly arrived when we needed them to fulfill God's call. When you give unbridled, you will experience unbridled response and blessing.

A giving heart toward the right soil, such as true prophetic ministry, can open a reward of the prophet's word to you and other miraculous provisions!

THE ANOINTING TO MULTIPLY

Prophets are representatives of the Voice of God. They carry a unique anointing to do the impossible. When you sow into it with honor, impossible break-throughs can happen in your life. Prophets carry an anointing for supernatural multiplication.

> *Then a man came from Baal Shalisha, and brought the man of God bread of the first-fruits, twenty loaves of barley bread, and newly ripened grain in his knapsack. And he said, "Give it to the people, that they may eat."* [43] *But his servant said, "What? Shall I set this before one hundred men?" He said again, "Give it to the people, that they may eat; for thus says the Lord: 'They shall eat and have some left over.'"* [44] *So he set it before them; and they ate and had some left over, according to the word of the Lord.*
>
> —2 Kings 4:42-44

One of the supernatural gifts God placed on the prophet is the anointing to multiply! When operated with purity, this is a potent force for the kingdom of God. We see this in 2 Kings 4:42, as the man from

Baal Shalisha, an area known for crops and having its harvest arrive before other areas.

WHAT BAAL SHALISHA REPRESENTS

Baal Shalisha represents:

1. Baal Shalisha represents a firstfruit offering placed at the feet of the prophet.
2. Baal was the god of selfish prosperity and mammon of the Old Testament. This offering was exchanging the wealth of the wicked to provide a miracle for the righteous.

The conduit was the prophet. When laid at his feet, the reward kicked in, and a miracle of multiplication transpired!

Jesus performed the same miracle when feeding the five thousand (*see* Matthew 14:13-21).

THE PROPHET'S REWARD IS A PROPHET'S RESPONSIBILITY

The prophet should be detached from offerings and personal monetary gain. Prophets must see themselves as a conduit, a servant through whom God's people can benefit and receive the reward through their vessel.

TRUE PROPHETS SOMETIMES SAY NO

Sometimes, the prophet must say no to gifts and special favors. The prophet must also purpose in his heart to be the most generous person people know. Extravagant generosity is the best way to stay clean regarding monetary gain.

A prophet who gives aggressively will *break the demon of mammon* from themselves and their ministry. Sowing aggressively is also rich soil that will produce a reward.

PERVERSION OF THE PROPHET'S REWARD

The Bible refers to Balaam's desire for personal gain as his *error*. Balaam wasn't a true prophet of God; he was into occultic practices, as no true prophet would dare curse the children of God or teach others how to defeat them.

Some believe Balaam was related to or was connected to Jannes and Jambres, the two diviner false prophets who resisted Moses.

BALAAM LOVED MONEY

The love of money drove Balaam's twistedness. Loving money is one of the biggest downfalls for any minister, or for that matter, any person.

When ministries use gimmicks for giving, such as a vial of water from some river or for sending X amount of money, you will get a prophecy—that is not the prophet's reward. These would be considered false prophets.

How a prophet handles the blessing of the reward on their life is a serious matter. False prophets sensationalize and merchandise on the prophet's reward. That is a very dangerous place to be.

MONEY ALONE IS A TOOL—MAMMON IS THE LOVE OF MONEY

> *No one can serve two masters; for either he will hate the one and love the other, or else he will be loyal to the one and despise the other. You cannot serve God and mammon.*
> —Matthew 6:24

THE DEVIL DOESN'T HAVE THE ANOINTING, SO HE USES MONEY

In my book, *Breaking Hell's Economy*, I deal extensively with the topic of mammon:

Mammon is a spirit, and it is the love of money. It takes hold of people and causes them to do whatever they must to get money. Mammon is evil, and it is the currency of hell's economy. It is a powerful revelation once you understand that the devil cannot operate under the anointing or through God's supernatural power of the Holy Spirit. He cannot function in the blessing; therefore, his substitute is mammon! He has enticed mankind to fall in love with money, which is a simple definition of mammon. Mammon creates a self-reliance that cuts God out of the picture and places self on the throne of your provision. This is the foundation of hell's economy.

The prophet's reward is a potent force the Holy Spirit uses to destroy the bondage to mammon. Prophets hate the love of money! By revelation, the spirit of faith will rise through legitimate prophets (who live what they preach) who teach on supernatural provision, and a breakthrough of resources will happen.

Real prophets understand the difference between the blessing and mammon. Proverbs 10:22 says, "The blessing of the Lord makes one rich, and He adds no sorrow with it." Preaching and radical giving induced by the prophet will break people into God's economy!

TAX MIRACLE

Jesus was more than a prophet, but when He spoke instruction like a prophet and those around Him listened to Him and responded, there was a reward. A prophetic miracle paid taxes!

> *Nevertheless, lest we offend them, go to the sea, cast in a hook, and take the fish that comes up first. And when you have opened its mouth, you will find a piece of money; take that and give it to them for Me and you.*
> —Matthew 17:27

DEBT FREEDOM

> *But as one was cutting down a tree, the iron ax head fell into the water; and he cried out and said, "Alas, master! For it was borrowed.* ⁶ *So the man of God said, "Where did it fall?"*

And he showed him the place. So he cut off a stick, and threw it in there; and he made the iron float.

—2 Kings 6:5-6

One day, a worker was cutting down a tree, and the iron head of his ax fell into the water. The man had a borrowed ax! He was in debt to the lender with potentially serious ramifications. Elisha did a prophetic act of faith and supernaturally resolved the man's debt! The prophet's reward has a debt-release ability!

SOWING IS THE BEST RESPONSE TO TROUBLE OR CRISIS

The prophet's reward is to be delivered supernaturally from lack in the middle of hardship or famine.

*So he arose and went to Zarephath. And when he came to the gate of the city, indeed a widow was there gathering sticks. And he called to her and said, "Please bring me a little water in a cup, that I may drink." *[11]* And as she was going to get it, he called to her and said, "Please bring me a morsel of bread in* *your hand."* ¹² *So she said, "As the Lord your God lives, I do not have bread, only a handful of flour in a bin, and a little oil in a jar; and see, I am gathering a couple of sticks that I may go in and prepare it for myself and my son, that we may eat it, and die."* ¹³ *And Elijah said to her, "Do not fear; go and do as you have said, but make me a small cake from it first, and bring it to me; and afterward make some for yourself and your son.* ¹⁴ *For thus says the Lord God of Israel: 'The bin of flour shall not be used up, nor shall the jar of oil run dry, until the day the Lord sends rain on the earth.'"* ¹⁵ *So she went away and did according to the word of Elijah; and she and he and her household ate for many days.* ¹⁶ *The bin of flour was not used up, nor did the jar of oil run dry, according to the word of the Lord which He spoke by Elijah.* ¹⁷ *Now it happened after these things that the son of the woman who owned the house became sick. And his sickness was so serious that there was no breath left in him.* ¹⁸ *So she said to Elijah, "What have I to do with you, O man of God? Have you come to me to bring my sin to*

*remembrance, and to kill my son?" *[19]* And he said to her, "Give me your son." So he took him out of her arms and carried him to the upper room where he was staying, and laid him on his own bed. *[20]* Then he cried out to the Lord and said, "O Lord my God, have You also brought tragedy on the widow with whom I lodge, by killing her son?" *[21]* And he stretched himself out on the child three times, and cried out to the Lord and said, "O Lord my God, I pray, let this child's soul come back to him." *[22]* Then the Lord heard the voice of Elijah; and the soul of the child came back to him, and he revived. And Elijah took the child and brought him down from the upper room into the house and gave him to his mother. *[23]* And Elijah said, "See, your son lives!" *[24]* Then the woman said to Elijah, "Now by this I know that you are a man of God, and that the word of the Lord in your mouth is the truth."*
—1 Kings 17:10-24

This is a powerful example of the prophet's reward. In the middle of a famine, Elijah requested that the woman give him the last of her food. Her obedience engaged the prophet's reward, causing miraculous provision for her and her son!

Additionally, we see that a second reward came through the prophet when the widow's son died and the prophet brought him back to life.

All of this was due to the widow of Zarephath giving a sacrificial offering to the prophet! The reward kept coming.

ELISHA AND THE PROPHET'S REWARD

This is mirrored in the story of Elisha in 2 Kings 4, with another widow in debt and the creditor was coming to take away her two sons. Interestingly, there was a miracle in the story where oil continued to flow from as many jars as the woman brought. The moment she stopped bringing the jars was when the oil stopped flowing. The prophet's reward will likely continue operating according to what you bring and by your faith. Had she kept bringing jars, the oil would have likely continued filling them!

Elisha also brought back the life of the Shulamite woman's son, again mirroring what Elijah had done years beforehand.

THE PROPHET'S REWARD FOREWARNS CALAMITY

> *And in these days prophets came from Jerusalem to Antioch.* ^{28} *Then one of them, named Agabus, stood up and showed by the Spirit that there was going to be a great famine throughout all the world, which also happened in the days of Claudius Caesar.* ^{29} *Then the disciples, each according to his ability, determined to send relief to the brethren dwelling in Judea.* ^{30} *This they also did, and sent it to the elders by the hands of Barnabas and Saul.*
>
> —Acts 11:27-30

Part of the prophet's reward is seeing evil coming and preparing for it. In the case of Agabus, the people heard the word he shared and made provision for the coming famine! They didn't tremble; rather, they acted.

> *A prudent man foresees evil and hides himself, but the simple pass on and are punished.*
> —Proverbs 22:3

When you release what you possess into the kingdom, the possibilities for what God can do become limitless. It takes supernatural empowerment to accomplish everything you are purposed to do in God's design. This does not happen by chance. We all have an active part in causing our lives to move forward.

In the areas of increase, it takes place through our giving, seeking first the kingdom with what we possess. Hebrews 7:8 says, "Here mortal men receive tithes, but there he receives them, of whom it is witnessed that he lives." This means we first give in the natural, but there is a corresponding action in the supernatural. When we choose to make it a priority to be a consistent giver, that corresponding action in the supernatural begins to spill over into our natural world.

IF YOU ENGAGE THE PROPHET'S REWARD, YOU ARE ENGAGING IN A SUPERNATURAL REACTION!

The prophet's reward is only one part of God's provision plan. Like a miracle worker who releases healing or a miraculous event in your life, the prophet's reward supplements walking in the blessing of the Lord through sowing.

> *So they rose early in the morning and went out into the Wilderness of Tekoa; and as they went out, Jehoshaphat stood and said, "Hear me, O Judah and you inhabitants of Jerusalem: Believe in the Lord your God, and you shall be established; believe His prophets, and you shall prosper."*
>
> —2 Chronicles 20:20

4

SACRIFICIAL GIVING CREATES RADICAL RETURNS

Something special happens when you give sacrificially for the gospel. The returns become radical.

In Mark 10:23, the Bible says, "Then Jesus looked around and said to His disciples, 'How hard it is for those who have riches to enter the kingdom of God!'" In the previous verses, Jesus told the rich young ruler he lacked one thing—to give to the poor and then follow Him.

For this young, wealthy man, that was a soul punch. So he walked away. Afterward, Jesus told His disciples it is hard for the rich to enter the kingdom of God. Scripture records in Mark 10:24 that the disciples were "astonished at His words."

For those whose riches come from their efforts and not the blessings of God, giving up everything on the altar becomes abhorrent. With that mindset, you cannot enter the kingdom of God or the righteousness, peace, and joy of God. However, when your riches come from God, no sorrow is added. Being wealthy, rich, and blessed by God is joyful.

Notice the difference between verses 23 and 24. In Mark 10:23, Jesus says, "How hard is it for those who *have riches* to enter the kingdom of God!" In Mark 10:24, Jesus says, "Children, how hard it is for those who *trust in riches* to enter the kingdom of God!" Do not miss the difference.

In verse 23, He's speaking of those who possess riches from their efforts. In verse 24, He's speaking of those who trust in riches to enter the kingdom of God. He is saying that people who trust their riches before they trust in God cannot enter heaven. Riches become their god.

In the next verse, Jesus expounds on the struggle for the rich. In Mark 10:25, He says, "It is easier for a camel to go through the eye of a needle than for a rich man to enter the kingdom of God." Some have surmised that this "eye of the needle" refers to a small gate in Jerusalem that a camel cannot get through while carrying its load. This is not true. There is no such gate. Jesus was creating a shocking image in the minds of His disciples. He refers to an actual needle and a real camel going through it. His point was that getting to God by trying harder isn't difficult—it's impossible!

People who trust in riches instead of God cannot enter the kingdom of God. First, they must lay it all down and surrender to Jesus; then, they will have access to the Father.

TRUST JESUS, NOT RICHES

Mark 10:26 says the disciples "were greatly astonished, saying among themselves, 'Who then can be saved?'" Why were they so concerned? Because they had financial means. They were fishermen and a tax collector.

They were businessmen who owned companies and assets, like boats. They probably worried that they couldn't be saved either. They misunderstood Jesus' words. He emphasized the difficulty for those who trust in riches, not those who possess them. "But Jesus looked at them and said, 'With men it is impossible, but not with God; for with God all things are possible'" (Mark 10:27). Jesus is telling us not to trust in our strength or wealth, but to trust in Him.

Upon hearing this, Peter pointed out to Jesus that he and the disciples had "left all and followed You."

Jesus put their sacrifice into a different perspective. In verse 29, He answered Peter, saying, "Assuredly, I say to you, there is no one who has left house or brothers or sisters or father or mother or wife or children or lands, for My sake and the gospel's."

There is something powerful that happens to those who sacrifice everything for the sake of the gospel. If the rich young man had trusted Jesus, he would have experienced it. He would have received back a hundred times what he gave. If he had given up everything to serve and trust Jesus by seeking the kingdom first, then all these things would have been added.

GIVE UP EVERYTHING FOR AND TO GOD

That's the secret to the hundredfold increase, which scripture mentions in Mark 10:30, "Who shall not receive a hundredfold now in this time—houses and brothers and sisters and mothers and children and lands, with persecutions—and in the age to come, eternal life." It's about letting go of what we're holding on to and embracing the gospel with both hands. We release the wealth we've acquired to receive the wealth God has planned. We must come to God with a pure heart and tell Him, "I'm leaving everything behind to serve You. I don't care what it costs me." That's when something supernatural happens.

Sadly, the rich young ruler never grasped what Jesus was saying. He wanted to give this young man more than he could imagine, but he had to willingly give it all up for Christ. Instead of telling him this, Jesus tested him. When he turned around and walked away, he walked away from Jesus and the hundred-fold blessings that were awaiting him.

Sacrificial giving for the sake of the gospel is one of the highest acts of worship while creating one of the highest forms of return. That level of giving is trust that cannot be faked. It is precious to the Lord, who has placed such a valuable reward for those who practice this selflessness.

BELIEVE GOD OVER YOUR EXPERIENCES

God wants you to win. Yes, there are sacrificial times when you must be willing to pour yourself out for the gospel. However, what should you do when you pour out and don't see a return?

You stand on the Word of God. You say, "Your Word is true. My heart and people's wisdom might lie, but God's Word does not. Your Word will perform and will come back to me." I've stood on this statement, and I've seen the overflow. He who began a good work in us is faithful to see it through to the end. You hold on to that promise, and you refuse to let go. This is the mindset we must grasp. We believe the Word of God over our experiences because persecution will come and try to steal the Word of God out of us.

FIND YOUR BIGGER VISION

In many churches where I minister, I see people with good hearts who are pacified with their gospel outreach. I love the body of Christ, but many members view their church and community as all there is. We need a bigger vision. If you want to prosper, think globally. You can't be "locally owned and globally minded," as many of my friends in business say. You've got to think about the greater body of Christ and how you can use your gifts to serve. We're not an island. Focusing inward is a sign of selfishness.

Over the years, I've had more people attack me over this message than anything else. But if you don't believe for increase in your life or seek to become a distribution center for the Word of God, you're insulting Jesus. It isn't until God stirs your heart and you start radically giving that you'll see the hundred-fold increase in your calling.

TAKE THAT FAITH LEAP

What about you? What's hindering your dream? The only thing that can hold you back is your mindset. You have to take a leap of faith. Unless you do, nothing will change.

This isn't about works. It's about encouraging you to step forward. If you struggle with the thought that God wants you to increase, you've either been mentored by poor teaching or you're carnally minded. Receiving abundance is not about getting. It's about increasing the kingdom of God. You are the body of Christ, and God wants His body to be prosperous. He wants the message of Jesus to go around the world. He needs you wealthy to achieve His goal.

5

LAST DAYS' WEALTH TRANSFER

For years, the terminology of *wealth transfer* has been thrown around. It sounds profound yet has produced very little substance. Here is why I believe that is. We are collectively the body of Christ, and within the body of Christ, there have been multimillionaires and even billionaires. In recent decades came the rise of "mega" churches and congregations. Even "para-church" Christian organizations have had tremendous amounts of wealth and resources. This is nothing special—a lot of money has gone through the body of Christ.

Yet the global impact of what "could be" has not yet matched what the Bible suggests—a worldwide shift in the axis of power. The components needed for this axis shift would be a global crisis and the righteous preemptively positioned in the *grace lane* they are called to walk in. Elements of crisis and alignment would set things up for a transition of power.

As far-fetched as something like this may sound, it is possible.

NOT THROUGH FORCE BUT THROUGH INFLUENCE

Influence is required to shine your light, but here is the issue—it requires God's people to seriously consider if they are where they are supposed to be. Questioning if you are where you are called to be is serious business and must be answered because it impacts nearly every part of your future. Many respond by saying, "I will do what God wants me to do; I just don't know how to find what that is or how even to begin."

Solutions for this issue are very present but require being a disciplined follower of Jesus through His Word and prayer. It may require a season of focused separation with Him. Most people sadly don't take their walk with the Lord seriously enough to discover His will for their lives. Every believer must intensely seek the Lord as if their whole life and destiny depend on it—because it does!

PURPOSE OF A WEALTH TRANSFER

An idea about wealth transfer: it's a large currency amount that we will buy into a new culture. It's a nice idea, but money alone doesn't solve the purpose of a wealth transfer. It must also be for a purpose and positioning. When looking at generational purpose rather than generational wealth, the narrative changes. It's vital that "purpose" be transferred to the next generation. Without it, the financial substance will only last as long as their consumer habits allow.

For decades, my wife and I have preached all around the world. During those travels, we encountered various individuals who held unique beliefs. Hearing someone tell us they will be a billionaire or exceedingly wealthy is common. There is nothing wrong with this type of belief, but usually, it comes from a well-meaning person who is broke and struggling to survive. I am not casting judgment on anyone; for many years, Heather and I were impoverished to the point of embarrassment. We sowed our way out and have since proved God's economy works if you will work it!

I'm talking about the believer living in the clouds; they are filled with wishful thinking. They are hoping for something toward which they have taken no steps of action, including no measurable steps to get into God's economy, such as tithing, sowing, or partnering with the preaching of the gospel. They don't do any of the necessary things and often don't have a steady job or any form of consistency to show their faithfulness. Yet they believe God will supernaturally hand them millions, billions, or even trillions of currency.

That mindset goes against the principles of God's Word regarding faithfulness and stewardship. The idea that one person will have trillions in currency, setting them up for whatever they want, is like a Holy Ghost lottery mentality. This is not to say a faithful person who sows and shows intense diligence can't experience a wild increase, favor, abundance, and more. However, it is still not God's highest and best.

It is vital to step away from pipe dreams about wealth transfer. Also, it's essential to understand that an increase on a personal level is not all there is. It will take far more than this to see significant change. The purpose of wealth transfer is to ultimately see the gospel go around the world through the corporate body of Christ. This is what God will supernaturally finance. Souls are His heartbeat and make Him rich.

INDIVIDUAL FAITHFULNESS LEADS TO CORPORATE VICTORY

And as they heard these things, he added and spake a parable, because he was nigh to

Jerusalem, and because they thought that the kingdom of God should immediately appear. ¹² *He said therefore, A certain nobleman went into a far country to receive for himself a kingdom, and to return.* ¹³ *And he called his ten servants, and delivered them ten pounds, and said unto them, Occupy till I come.* ¹⁴ *But his citizens hated him, and sent a message after him, saying, We will not have this man to reign over us.*

¹⁵ *And it came to pass, that when he was returned, having received the kingdom, then he commanded these servants to be called unto him, to whom he had given the money, that he might know how much every man had gained by trading.* ¹⁶ *Then came the first, saying, Lord, thy pound hath gained ten pounds.* ¹⁷ *And he said unto him, Well, thou good servant: because thou hast been faithful in a very little, have thou authority over ten cities.* ¹⁸ *And the second came, saying, Lord, thy pound hath gained five pounds.* ¹⁹ *And he said likewise to him, Be thou also over five cities.*

²⁰ And another came, saying, Lord, behold, here is thy pound, which I have kept laid up in a napkin: ²¹ for I feared thee, because thou art an austere man: thou takest up that thou layedst not down, and reapest that thou didst not sow. ²² And he saith unto him, Out of thine own mouth will I judge thee, thou wicked servant. Thou knewest that I was an austere man, taking up that I laid not down, and reaping that I did not sow: ²³ wherefore then gavest not thou my money into the bank, that at my coming I might have required mine own with usury?

²⁴ And he said unto them that stood by, Take from him the pound, and give it to him that hath ten pounds. ²⁵ (And they said unto him, Lord, he hath ten pounds.) ²⁶ For I say unto you, That unto every one which hath shall be given; and from him that hath not, even that he hath shall be taken away from him. ²⁷ But those mine enemies, which would not that I should reign over them, bring hither, and slay them before me.

—Luke 19:11-27 KJV

Luke 19:11-27 is the parable of the ten minas (pounds). Notice that the reward for being faithful with the portion given them was equal to what they would receive in return. It is also fascinating to understand that the nobleman wanted increase on what he invested and turned over to each individual. The nobleman also sized them up according to what he knew they could handle and produce and their capacity for responsibility. When one of them did not produce what the nobleman knew he could, this caused issues.

Points we can learn from this:

1. The nobleman invested in what he knew they could handle.
2. The nobleman wanted a return on his investment.
3. The reward for good stewardship was territory.
4. The one who failed the stewardship test had his financial holding given to the one with the most.
5. How the individual with only one mina viewed the nobleman was how the nobleman treated him in return.

The way you view God is how you may receive from Him. It is our responsibility to be good stewards of what we are given. This, in turn, leads to picking up the investment given to the unfaithful. The reward of good stewardship is territory and responsibility. How does this apply to a wealth transfer? When you become positioned and are a good steward, you increase what God gives you, and a reward of territory and responsibility comes into your possession.

If you do what is prescribed, you will take territory by the hand of God. Unite this action of one individual with the actions of many who do the same thing. What will happen? Major territory is taken corporately as the body of Christ. Ultimately, we will be positioned through good stewardship to reap territory, cities, and more. Biblically, this is how the fundamentals of a corporate anointing work. Many individuals today most likely would keep increasing for their benefit and giving to this or that cause along the way. Although there is nothing wrong with this and it is most likely how the vast majority would handle their increase, hell's economy would be destroyed and never recover if the corporate body of Christ applied the principles in Luke 19:11-27.

Faithfulness in what you have and unity with other like-minded believers who have the same experience will destroy hell's economy. I believe this is possible in a *last-days'* wealth transfer.

GOD DESIRES A UNIFIED BODY

God is looking for a unified body. I believe a wealth transfer will only be to the magnitude of a unified body.

A unified body of believers on a large scale would, by default, release an unprecedented wealth transfer and a miraculous supernatural shift in the culture. In a crisis, with people coming unglued worldwide, we are anointed to be the solid lighthouse people run to. As a united body, we would offer hope and stability.

We are in a time when everyone is looking for answers—when markets inevitably will crumble, institutions will fail, and the world will go into turmoil. We, the body of Christ, will have an opportunity to be positioned and draw all those desperate to escape the chaos into a place of peace.

This generation or a future generation can step into a position of influence and financial authority as a united global superpower. Every generation has this opportunity, but who will take it? Even if the body of Christ rises and it is not to be attained in our generation, that doesn't mean it's not possible. I believe the absolute will of God will come to pass no matter what. However, there is also the opportunity God gives us.

JESUS MARVELED
AT EXCEPTIONAL FAITH

In the account recorded in Matthew 8:5-13, the centurion soldier says in verses 8-9, "But only speak a word, and my servant will be healed. [9] For I also am a man under authority, having soldiers under me. And I say to this one, 'Go,' and he goes; and to another, 'Come,' and he comes." Verse 10 says, "When Jesus heard it, He marveled, and said to those who followed, 'Assuredly, I say to you, I have not found such great faith, not even in Israel!'"

What a statement by Jesus! This means that instances like the centurion or the woman with the issue of blood have meaning. The woman with the issue of blood, in Mark 5:25-34, reached out and took hold of Jesus' garment, evoking a response from Him: "Who touched me?" She said within herself, "If I can touch the hem of His garment, I will be made well." When you apply radical, fully persuaded faith toward anything from God, it will get His attention! You can make such a draw on what is available that even Jesus might be surprised.

There are moments when we can stretch our faith based on His Word. Through this, tremendous things can happen. I believe the Lord loves over-the-top, faith-filled actions demonstrated by us toward Him.

Along with faithfulness, sowing, and steward-ship, this kind of faith is required to see the impossible happen! You will only receive to the level you believe. A wealth transfer is not necessary or a commandment, much like receiving blessings, healings, or anything the Word of God says we can have. It is something that must be pursued by revelation. The key element is corporate unification. With that in place, a *last-days'* wealth transfer is possible.

JOSEPH AND HIS GENERATION'S WEALTH TRANSFER

So when the money failed in the land of Egypt and in the land of Canaan, all the Egyptians came to Joseph and said, "Give us bread, for why should we die in your presence? For the money has failed."

—Genesis 47:15

Joseph was prepared for the seven years of fam-ine. He was positioned to make Egypt the most powerful nation in the world, but only to take what they had accumulated. "The wealth of the wicked is stored up for the righteous." Joseph brought this prophetic scripture to pass by his obedience to God. The seven years forced all the surrounding peoples and nations to give over their money, food, and finally, themselves. This changed the day God's people left Egypt with all the gold, silver, and precious things. The wealth of Egypt was stored up for the righteous— those who had covered their doors with blood and had survived the ten plagues. These individuals were the recipients of what was accumulated during the time of Joseph. Generational purpose was in place for the exodus of God's people to go into the land of promise.

THE WORD OF THE LORD TESTED JOSEPH

Until the time that his word came to pass, the word of the Lord tested him.
—Psalm 105:19

Of the utmost importance, you need to remember that Joseph spent years of his life not seeing what he was promised. It was a test for him, carrying his

God-given dream while he experienced the opposite of what the Lord promised. Due to his tenacity and resilience, Joseph spent years being positioned until finally his day came. This resulted from refusing to falter on what the Lord showed him in his dreams as a boy. The takeaway: Do not faint. It will come to pass if you have the staying power and selflessness to see it through!

WHAT A WEALTH TRANSFER LOOKS LIKE

Isaiah 60 gives a glimpse of what a global wealth transfer might look like.

> *Arise, shine; for your light has come! And the glory of the Lord is risen upon you. ² For behold, the darkness shall cover the earth, and deep darkness the people; but the Lord will arise over you, and His glory will be seen upon you. ³ The Gentiles shall come to your light, and kings to the brightness of your rising. ⁴ Lift up your eyes all around, and see: they all gather together, they come to you; your sons shall come from afar, and your daughters shall be nursed at your side.*

⁵ *Then you shall see and become radiant, and your heart shall swell with joy; because the abundance of the sea shall be turned to you, the wealth of the Gentiles shall come to you.* ⁶ *The multitude of camels shall cover your land, the dromedaries of Midian and Ephah; all those from Sheba shall come; they shall bring gold and incense, and they shall proclaim the praises of the Lord.* ⁷ *All the flocks of Kedar shall be gathered together to you, the rams of Nebaioth shall minister to you; they shall ascend with acceptance on My altar, and I will glorify the house of My glory.*

—Isaiah 60:1-7

GLOBAL DARKNESS

Isaiah 60:2 talks about *darkness covering the earth and the people*. This describes a time of crisis, and it is in times such as this when opportunity arises. This is likely the description of a global darkness, a crippling terror much like the darkness that covered Egypt for three days. During this time, darkness is not only covering the earth! It covers the people and the earth. This darkness is twofold.

1. Darkness that covers the people is the removal of light or revelation. Romans 1:21 says, "Because, although they knew God, they did not glorify Him as God, nor were thankful, but became futile in their thoughts, and their foolish hearts were darkened." Psalm 27 also refers to the Lord as light. First John additionally says God is light. This reference to darkness is the removal of God from thinking, society, and their believing. It is a complete perversion of the mind and culture.

2. This is a full manifestation of the gates of hell setting up its nefarious system on a global scale—a cultural darkness unlike anything the world has seen before. This may refer to a literal darkness as well. What we can see is that this darkness impacts the entirety of the planet.

THE LORD WILL ARISE

The Lord will counter the darkness by rising. How does God rise? Over you! By causing His glory to be seen upon you. This may be describing a literal glow on the people of God, like the face of Moses when he returned from the mountain. It will be a distinction from the darkness that prevails on the earth then. Pure light shining through the righteous on that day will cause a reaction. Gentiles will be drawn to this light, to the brightness of your rising. Believers will be put on display.

It will be on both Gentiles and kings, average people worldwide (Gentiles) and those in authority (kings). A revelation comes upon the people of God in Isaiah 60:5, saying, "You shall see and become radiant, and your heart shall swell with joy; because…"

GLOBAL WEALTH TRANSFER

"…the abundance of the sea shall be turned toward you; the wealth of the Gentiles shall come to you." The term *abundance of the sea* is important. The "sea" throughout the Word of God is often a direct reference to the nations, all the different types of people and ethnic groups worldwide. In this passage, *sea* describes what someone could argue was the entire world population. It goes on to say "*the* wealth of *the* Gentiles." Notice it doesn't say *Gentiles* generally; it uses the definite article twice: "*the* wealth of *the* Gentiles shall come to you." It doesn't leave much room for thinking something other than the wealth of the Gentiles. *Gentiles* refers to everyone and every nation outside of God's kingdom. They will not only come to you, but all the wealth they possess will also come to you—whether they bring wealth or not.

Whether the unbelievers, wicked people, or those in darkness willingly or unwillingly bring their wealth, this picture portrays the world's wealth as coming to you. A transfer is happening here. When Isaiah 60:5 describes seeing this and becoming radiant and your heart swelling with joy, I'm reminded of Proverbs 10:22: "The blessing of the Lord makes one rich, and He adds no sorrow with it."

The blessing of the Lord is behind this wealth transfer because only the blessing causes a heart swelling with joy and radiance! God is behind this transfer. "The wealth of the Gentiles shall come to you" is a result of the blessing because the blessing "makes" one rich. Even into the rest of Isaiah 60, the remaining verses deal with the belongings and ownership of the received wealth.

HELL'S ECONOMY HAS PRIORITIES IN REVERSE

Therefore do not worry, saying, "What shall we eat?" or "What shall we drink?" or "What shall we wear?" [32] *For after all these things the Gentiles seek. For your heavenly Father knows that you need all these things. [33] But seek first the kingdom of God and His righteousness, and all these things shall be added to you.*

—Matthew 6:31-33

Gentiles, unbelievers, those who are rooted in hell's economy seek "things." They don't seek spiritual truth because they cannot discern it. They are not seekers of God's kingdom, as Matthew 6:33 says. Gentiles seek what they will eat, drink, and what they can wear. In other words, they seek "stuff "—physical needs and comforts. They desire monetary means that will provide them with the things they seek. As believers, we are not to seek these things; instead, we are to seek the kingdom of God and His righteousness, and then all these "things" will be added unto us.

This is a place of positioning. How do you *seek first* the "kingdom" to be positioned? Through being where God has called you to be and by sowing seed. In proper order with the kingdom of God as priority, you will supernaturally have all these other things added to you. Remember, the blessing makes one rich! The blessing makes these things—what you shall eat, drink, and wear (and everything you desire in line with God's Word)—come to you.

GENTILES, COME TO YOUR LIGHT

Isaiah 60 references the Gentiles coming to your light! The Gentiles will one day come to God's people because they see a light on you in a world of darkness and because you possess all the things they seek. You will own all their stuff!

The greatest wealth transfers always occur during famine and crises. As Isaiah 60 states, "Darkness shall cover the land, and deep darkness shall the people." Yet, God's economy hides surprising wealth for those who enter its system.

A good man leaves an inheritance to his children's children, but the wealth of the sinner is stored up for the righteous.

—Proverbs 13:22

I will give you the treasures of darkness and hidden riches of secret places, that you may know that I, the Lord, who call you by your name, am the God of Israel.

—Isaiah 45:3

For the earth will be filled with the knowledge of the glory of the Lord, as the waters cover the sea.

—Habakkuk 2:14

Once again, the sea refers to people from all around the world—every tribe, tongue, and nation. Habakkuk 2:14 alludes to the knowledge of the glory of the Lord covering the earth as the waters cover the sea or all the people on earth. God's end goal is to have the gospel reach every person, and that is what the knowledge of the glory of the Lord means.

If you support that and position yourself on God's path, you will be prepared for a potential end-time wealth transfer. The body of Christ is called to change the world! You are called to take your place in history by participating in the corporate body of Christ. Your life is needed now more than ever, and you mean more to the big picture than you might realize.

God wants to bless you beyond your wildest imagination. You will reap a prophet's reward when you sow into a prophet and good soil. This can come as a wealth transfer. The enemy wants to steal from you, but God desires to pour abundance into all areas of your life.

*The thief does not come except to steal, and to kill, and to destroy. I have come that they may have life, and that they may have it more **abundantly**.*

—John 10:10

About Joseph Z

Joseph Z is an author, broadcaster, Bible teacher, and international prophetic voice. Before the age of nine, he began encountering the Voice of God through dreams and visions. Joseph has dedicated his life to preaching the gospel around the world. He and his wife, Heather, are founders of Z Ministries, a media and conference-based ministry in Colorado, USA.

FOR FURTHER INFORMATION

If you would like prayer or further information about Joseph Z Ministries, please call our offices at

(719) 257-8050 or visit **JosephZ.com/contact**

Visit JosephZ.com
for additional materials.

www.ingramcontent.com/pod-product-compliance
Lightning Source LLC
Chambersburg PA
CBHW071638040426
42452CB00009B/1680